To

Maureen
_____

From

Eddie + Mary-Ellen
For your 50th Birthday!!

365 DAY BRIGHTENERS™

Celebrating Friendship

GARBORG'S®

because every day is a gift

365 Day Brighteners™ Celebrating Friendship

Copyright © 2004 DaySpring® Cards, Inc.
Published by Garborg's®, a brand of DaySpring® Cards, Inc.
Siloam Springs, Arkansas
www.dayspring.com

ISBN 1-58061-789-1

Printed in China

365 DAY BRIGHTENERS™

Celebrating
Friendship

To have a good friend is one of the highest delights of life; to be a good friend is one of the noblest and most difficult undertakings.

January 1

$\mathcal{M}$y friend shall forever be my
friend and reflect a ray of God to me.

HENRY DAVID THOREAU

One of the blessings of friendship comes from our
joy in discovering God's grace and purpose for
bringing us into each other's lives.

January 2

$\mathcal{T}$here is no wilderness like a life without friends; friendship multiplies blessings and minimizes misfortunes; it is a unique remedy against adversity, and it soothes the soul.

BALTASAR GRACIAN

January 3

*I*f I can soothe the way for you,
and you help me along,
Won't we both have greater joy
and keep each other strong?

January 4

*D*ear friends, let us practice loving each other, for love comes from God and those who are loving and kind show that they are the children of God, and that they are getting to know him better.

1 JOHN 4:7 TLB

January 5

$\mathcal{T}$oday a man discovered gold and fame,
Another flew the stormy seas,
Another set an unarmed world aflame,
One found the germ of a disease.
But what high fates my path attend,
For I —today—I found a friend.

HELEN BARKER PARKER

January 6

A friend is a precious possession
whose value increases with years,
Someone who does not forsake us
when a difficult moment appears.

HENRY VAN DYKE

January 7

*N*othing opens the heart like a true friend, to whom you may impart griefs, joys, fears, hopes and whatever lies upon the heart.

FRANCIS BACON

January 8

Sincerity is when you listen with your heart, truth when you speak with love, and faithfulness when you walk beside me, whatever life brings my way. Friendship is the gift of Grace that makes all of those things possible.

January 9

Therefore, as God's chosen people, holy and dearly loved, clothe yourselves with compassion, kindness, humility, gentleness and patience. Bear with each other and forgive whatever grievances you may have against one another. Forgive as the Lord forgave you. And over all these virtues put on love, which binds them all together in perfect unity.

COLOSSIANS 3:12-14 NIV

January 10

$\mathcal{F}$riends…cherish each other's
hopes…and are kind
to each other's dreams.

HENRY DAVID THOREAU

*Life is what we are alive to. It is not length
but breadth…Be alive to…goodness,
kindness, purity, love, history, poetry, music,
flowers, stars, God, and eternal hope.*

MALTBIE D. BABCOCK

January 11

$\mathcal{T}$he secret of life is that all we have
and are is a gift of grace to be shared.

LLOYD JOHN OGILVIE

*Not only does understanding the gospel of the
grace of God provide a proper motive for us to
share our faith, it also gives us the proper motive
and means to live the Christian life effectively.*

DAVID HOWARD

January 12

$\mathscr{L}$ove comes out of heaven
unasked and unsought.

PEARL S. BUCK

*Be on the lookout for mercies. The more we look
for them, the more of them we will see…. Better to
lose count while naming your blessings than to
lose your blessings to counting your troubles.*

January 13

God, who is love, simply cannot help but shed blessing upon blessing upon us. We do not need to beg, for He simply cannot help it.

HANNAH WHITHALL SMITH

January 14

$\mathcal{N}$ow there are different kinds of spiritual gifts, but it is the same Holy Spirit who is the source of them all. There are different kinds of service in the church, but it is the same Lord we are serving. There are different ways God works in our lives, but it is the same God who does the work through all of us. A spiritual gift is given to each of us as a means of helping the entire church.

1 CORINTHIANS 12: 4-7 NLT

January 15

Having someone who understands
is a great blessing for ourselves.
Being someone who understands
is a great blessing to others.

JANETTE OKE

January 16

Blessed are they who have the gift of making friends, for it is one of God's best gifts. It involves many things, but above all, the power of getting out of one's self, and appreciating whatever is noble and loving in another.

THOMAS HUGHES

January 17

*H*uman beings are born into this little span of life of which the best thing is its friendships and intimacies…and yet they leave their friendships and intimacies with no cultivation, to grow as they will by the roadside, expecting them to "keep" by force of mere inertia.

WILLIAM JAMES

January 18

$\mathcal{L}$ead the life that will make you kindly and friendly to everyone about you, and you will be surprised what a happy life you will live.

CHARLES M. SCHWAB

January 19

*A*fter David finished talking with Saul,
he met Jonathan, the king's son.
There was an immediate bond
of love between them, and they
became the best of friends.

1 SAMUEL 18:1 NLT

January 20

$\mathscr{T}$he greatest gift you can give another is
your undivided attention.

*There is a definite process by which one made
people into friends, and it involved talking to them
and listening to them for hours at a time.*

REBECCA WEST

January 21

$\mathcal{T}$here is no real distance between true friends, for they are always connected heart-to-heart.

I am learning to live close to the lives of my friends without ever seeing them. No miles of any measurement can separate your soul from mine.

JOHN MUIR

January 22

$\mathcal{W}$hat the heart keeps in memory of
gracious sharing, kindness, caring…gifts
true friends have shown,
Never fades and never sleeps, and never
stands alone.

January 23

$\mathcal{F}$riends reflect the best in each other.

*The only service a friend can really render
is to keep up your courage by holding up
to you a mirror in which you can see
a noble image of yourself.*

GEORGE BERNARD SHAW

January 24

$\mathcal{L}$et us hold unswervingly to the hope
we profess, for he who promised is
faithful. And let us consider how we may
spur one another on toward love and
good deeds. Let us not give up meeting
together, as some are in the habit of
doing, but let us encourage one another.

HEBREWS 10:23-25 NIV

January 25

$\mathcal{T}$he way to make a true friend is to be one. Friendship implies loyalty, esteem, cordiality, sympathy, affection, readiness to aid, to help, to stick, to fight for, if need be...radiate friendship and it will return sevenfold.

B. C. FORBES

January 26

One whose grip is a little tighter,
One whose smile is a little brighter,
One whose deeds are a little whiter,
that's what I call a friend.

JOHN BURROUGHS

January 27

$\mathcal{D}$on't walk behind me,
I may not lead.
Don't walk in front of me,
I may not follow.
Just walk beside me
and be my friend.

ALBERT CAMUS

January 28

$\mathcal{S}$ometimes our light goes out but is blown into flame by another human being. Each of us owes the deepest thanks to those who have rekindled this light.

ALBERT SCHWEITZER

January 29

Two are better than one, because they
have a good return for their work:
If one falls down, his friend can help
him up. But pity the man who falls
and has no one to help him up!

ECCLESIASTES 4:9-10 NIV

January 30

$\mathcal{S}$o long as we love, we serve; so long as we are loved by others I would almost say that we are indispensable; and no man is useless while he has a friend.

ROBERT LOUIS STEVENSON

January 31

You will find, as you look back on your life, that...the moments when you have really lived are the moments when you have done things in the spirit of love.

HENRY DRUMMOND

February 1

$\mathcal{F}$riendship is born at that moment when one person says to another: "What? You, too? I thought I was the only one."

C. S. LEWIS

$\mathcal{F}$*ebruary 2*

A true friend is one who is concerned about what we are becoming, who sees beyond the present relationship, and who cares deeply about us as a whole person.

GLORIA GAITHER

February 3

To know someone here or there
with whom you feel there is an
understanding in spite of distances
or thoughts unexpressed...that can
make of this earth a garden.

GOETHE

February 4

$\mathcal{M}$ay the Lord bless and protect you;
may the Lord's face radiate with joy
because of you; may he be gracious
to you, show you his favor,
and give you his peace.

NUMBERS 6:24-26 TLB

February 5

$\mathcal{F}$riendship: It involves many things but, above all, the power of going out of one's self and seeing and appreciating whatever is noble and loving in another.

THOMAS HUGHES

$\mathcal{F}ebruary$ 6

$\mathcal{S}$ometimes being a friend means mastering the art of timing. There is a time for silence. A time to let go and allow people to hurl themselves into their own destiny. And a time to prepare to pick up the pieces when it's all over.

OCTAVIA BUTLER

$\mathcal{F}ebruary$ 7

*H*ave you had a kindness shown?
Pass it on! 'Twas not given for thee alone,
Pass it on! Let it travel down the years,
Let it wipe another's tears, Till in Heaven
the deed appears—Pass it on!

HENRY BURTON

February 8

Be such a [one], and live such a life,
that if every [one] were such as you,
and every life a life like yours,
this earth would be God's Paradise.

PHILLIPS BROOKS

February 9

Shout for joy to the Lord, all the earth.
Worship the Lord with gladness;
come before him with joyful songs.
Know that the Lord is God. It is he
who made us, and we are his; we are
his people, the sheep of his pasture.
Enter his gates with thanksgiving
and his courts with praise; give
thanks to him and praise his name.
For the Lord is good and his love
endures forever; his faithfulness
continues through all generations.

PSALM 100 NIV

February 10

The true way and the sure way
to friendship is through humility, being
open to each other, accepting each other
just as we are, knowing each other.

MOTHER TERESA

February 11

*T*here is nothing we like to see
so much as the gleam of pleasure
in a person's eye when he feels that
we have sympathized with him,
understood him, [become] interested
in his welfare. At these moments
something fine and spiritual passes
between two friends. These moments
are the moments worth living.

DON MARQUIS

February 12

*G*iving encouragement to others
is a most welcome gift, for the results
of it are lifted spirits, Increased
self-worth, and a hopeful future.

FLORENCE LITTAUER

February 13

Do not keep the alabaster boxes of your love and tenderness sealed up until your friends are dead. Fill their lives with sweetness. Speak approving cheering words while their ears can hear them and while their hearts can be thrilled by them.

HENRY WARD BEECHER

February 14

$\mathcal{F}$or the life of every living thing is in his hand, and the breath of all humanity. Just as the mouth tastes good food, so the ear tests the words it hears. Wisdom belongs to the aged, and understanding to those who have lived many years.

JOB 12:10-12 NLT

February 15

$\mathcal{W}$hen thoughts we share become a
seed, that grows and helps fulfill a need,
They tend to blossom in the heart,
creating friends who'll never part.

$\mathcal{F}ebruary\ 16$

True friends don't spend time gazing into each other's eyes. They may show great tenderness towards each other, but they face in the same direction—toward common projects, goals—above all, towards a common Lord.

C. S. LEWIS

February 17

$\mathcal{T}$he more we love, the better we are,
and the greater our friendships are,
the dearer we are to God.

JEREMY TAYLOR

$\mathcal{F}$ebruary 18

*H*elp us to help each other, Lord,
Each other's cross to bear,
Let each his friendly aid afford,
And feel his brother's care.

CHARLES WESLEY

February 19

Our lives are a medley of joy and tears,
hope and help, love and encouragement.

*Be full of sympathy toward each other, loving one
another with tender hearts and humble minds.*

1 PETER 3:8 TLB

February 20

$\mathcal{N}$o medicine is more valuable,
none more efficacious, none better
suited to the cure of all our temporal
ills than a friend to whom we may
turn for consolation in time of
trouble—and with whom we may
share our happiness in time of joy.

AELRED OF RIEVAULX

February 21

*L*ove is extravagant in the price it is willing to pay, the time it is willing to give, the hardships it is willing to endure, and the strength it is willing to spend.

JONI EARECKSON TADA

February 22

*O*rder your soul; reduce your wants;
live in charity; associate in Christian
community, obey the laws;
trust in Providence.

AUGUSTINE

February 23

*F*ortify yourself with a flock of friends!
You can select them at random, write to
one, dine with one, visit one, or take your
problems to one. There is always at least
one who will understand, inspire, and
give you the lift you need at the time.

GEORGE MATTHEW ADAMS

February 24

*D*ear brothers and sisters, I close my letter with these last words: Rejoice. Change your ways. Encourage each other. Live in harmony and peace. Then the God of love and peace will be with you. Greet each other in Christian love.

2 CORINTHIANS 13:11-12 NLT

February 25

The best in me and the best in you,
Hailed each other because they knew
That always and always since life began,
Our being friends was part of God's plan.

GEORGE WEBSTER DOUGLAS

February 26

$\mathcal{T}$he best and most beautiful
things in the world cannot
be seen or even touched.
They must be felt with the heart.

HELEN KELLER

February 27

Give strength, give thought,
give deeds, give wealth;
Give love, give tears, and give thyself.
Give, give, be always giving.
Who gives not is not living;
The more you give, the more you live.

February 28

No distance of place or lapse
of time can lessen the friendship
of those who are thoroughly
persuaded of each other's worth.

Robert Southey

February 29

$\mathcal{A}$nd do not grieve the Holy Spirit of God, with whom you were sealed for the day of redemption. Get rid of all bitterness, rage and anger, brawling and slander, along with every form of malice. Be kind and compassionate to one another, forgiving each other, just as in Christ God forgave you.

EPHESIANS 4:30-32 NIV

March 1

*H*uman comfort and divine comfort are of different natures: human comfort consists in external, visible help, which a man may see, hold, and feel; divine comfort only in words and promises, where there is neither seeing, hearing, nor feeling.

MARTIN LUTHER

March 2

A Christian should always remember that the value of his good works is not based on their number and excellence, but on the love of God which prompts him to do these things.

JOHN OF THE CROSS

March 3

To be glad of life, because it gives you the chance to love and to work and to play and to look up at the stars; to be satisfied with your possessions, but not contented with yourself until you have made the best of them; to despise nothing in the world except falsehood and meanness, and to fear nothing except cowardice;...to think seldom of your enemies, often of your friends, and every day of Christ; and to spend as much time as you can, with body and with spirit, in God's out-of-doors—these are little guideposts on the footpath to peace.

HENRY VAN DYKE

March 4

$\mathcal{M}$y command is this: Love each other as I have loved you. Greater love has no man than this, that he lay down his life for his friends. You are my friends if you do what I command.

JOHN 15:15 NIV

March 5

$\mathcal{T}$he happiness of life is made up of minute fractions—the little, soon-forgotten charities of a kiss or smile, a kind look, a heart-felt compliment, and the countless infinitesimals of pleasurable and genial feeling.

SAMUEL TAYLOR COLERIDGE

March 6

$\mathcal{T}$o be kind to all, to like many
and love a few, to be needed and
wanted by those we love, is certainly
the nearest we can come to happiness.

MARY ROBERTS RINEHART

March 7

Love is a great thing, an altogether
good gift, the only thing that
makes burdens light and bears
all that is hard with ease.

THOMAS À KEMPIS

March 8

$\mathcal{I}$'m not happy, I'm cheerful. There's a difference. A happy woman has no cares at all. A cheerful woman has cares but has learned how to deal with them.

BEVERLY SILLS

March 9

*O*h, the joys of those who trust the Lord, who have no confidence in the proud, or in those who worship idols. O Lord my God, you have done many miracles for us. Your plans for us are too numerous to list. If I tried to recite all your wonderful deeds, I would never come to the end of them.

PSALM 40:4-5 NLT

March 10

The happiness for which our souls ache is one undisturbed by success or failure, one which will root deeply inside us and give inward relaxation, peace, and contentment, no matter what the surface problems may be. That kind of happiness stands in need of no outward stimulus.

BILLY GRAHAM

March 11

J Jesus

O Others
Y Yourself
If you use the joy rule and think
of Jesus, then others, then yourself;
you will really feel true joy.

March 12

$\mathcal{T}$o have a good friend is the purest
of all God's gifts, for it is a love that
has no exchange of payment.

FRANCES FARMER

March 13

$\mathcal{C}$heerfulness is among the most
laudable virtues. It gains you
the good will and friendship of others.
It blesses those who practice it and
those upon whom it is bestowed.

B. C. FORBES

March 14

$\mathcal{B}$ut I tell you: Love your enemies
and pray for those who persecute you,
that you may be sons of your Father
in heaven. He causes his sun to rise on
the evil and the good, and sends rain on
the righteous and the unrighteous.
If you love those who love you,
what reward will you get? Are not
even the tax collectors doing that?

MATTHEW 5:44-46 NIV

March 15

Thank God for dirty dishes;
they have a tale to tell.
While other folks go hungry,
we're eating pretty well.
With home, and health, and happiness,
we shouldn't want to fuss;
For by this stack of evidence,
God's very good to us.

March 16

$\mathcal{T}$hree things in human life
are important: The first is to be kind.
The second is to be kind.
And the third is to be kind.

HENRY JAMES

March 17

$\mathcal{I}$ was hungered, and ye gave me meat;
I was thirsty, and ye gave me drink:
I was a stranger, and ye took me in:
I was naked, and ye clothed me:
I was sick, and ye visited me:
I was in prison, and ye came unto me.

March 18

It was only a sunny smile,
And little it cost in the giving,
But like morning light,
it scattered the night,
And made the day worth living.

March 19

Friends warm you with their presence, trust you with their secrets, and remember you in their prayers.

A word fitly spoken is like apples of gold in settings of silver.

PROVERBS 25:11 NKJV

March 20

$\mathcal{A}$ friend is able to see you as the wonderful person God created you to be.

ANN D. PARRISH

March 21

$\mathcal{E}$very day we live is a priceless gift of God, loaded with possibilities to learn something new, to gain fresh insights.

DALE EVANS ROGERS

March 22

$\mathcal{I}$f two friends ask you to judge
a dispute, don't accept, because you
will lose one friend; on the other hand,
if two strangers come with the
same request, accept, because
you will gain one friend.

AUGUSTINE

March 23

*O*ur happiness is greatest when we contribute to the happiness of others.

HARRIET SHEPARD

One thing I know: the only ones among you who will be really happy are those who will have sought and found how to serve.

ALBERT SCHWEITZER

March 24

Carry each other's burdens, and in this way you will fulfill the law of Christ. If anyone thinks he is something when he is nothing, he deceives himself. Each one should test his own actions. Then he can take pride in himself, without comparing himself to somebody else, for each one should carry his own load.

GALATIANS 6:2-5 NIV

March 25

Sunshine is delicious, rain is refreshing,
wind braces us up, snow is exhilarating;
there is really no such thing as bad
weather, only different kinds
of good weather.

JOHN RUSKIN

March 26

$\mathcal{I}$ expect to pass through this life but once. If, therefore, there be any kindness I can show, or any good thing I can do for any fellow being, let me do it now…as I shall not pass this way again.

WILLIAM PENN

March 27

$\mathcal{P}$rayer in action is love, and love in action is service. Try to give unconditionally whatever a person needs in the moment. The point is to do something, however small, and show you care through your actions by giving your time.

MOTHER TERESA

March 28

$\mathcal{W}$hen you get into a tight place
and everything goes against you, 'til it
seems as though you could not hold
on a minute longer, never give up then,
for that is just the place and time
that the tide will turn.

HARRIET BEECHER STOWE

March 29

$\mathcal{P}$ray for the happiness of those who curse you. Pray for those who hurt you. If someone slaps you on one cheek, turn the other cheek. If someone demands your coat, offer your shirt also. Give what you have to anyone who asks you for it; and when things are taken away from you, don't try to get them back. Do for others as you would like them to do for you.

LUKE 6:28-31 NLT

March 30

Silences make the real conversations between friends. Not the saying, but the never needing to say is what counts.

MARGARET LEE RUNBECK

March 31

Scatter seeds of kindness
everywhere you go;
Scatter bits of courtesy—
watch them grow and grow.
Gather buds of friendship,
keep them till full-blown;
You will find more happiness than you
have ever known.

AMY R. RAABE

April 1

$\mathcal{I}$t is great to have friends when one is young, but indeed it is still more so when you are getting old. When we are young, friends are, like everything else, a matter of course. In the old days we know what it means to have them.

EDVARD GRIEG

April 2

$\mathcal{I}$t is around the table that friends
understand best the warmth
of being together.

Italian saying:
*Come for dinner, or just tea, it doesn't
matter much to me, it's just that I must
simply be—somewhere close to you!*

April 3

The friend of my adversity I shall always cherish most. I can better trust those who helped to relieve the gloom of my dark hours than those who are so ready to enjoy with me the sunshine of my prosperity.

ULYSSES S. GRANT

April 4

The God who made the world and everything in it is the Lord of heaven and earth and does not live in temples built by hands. And he is not served by human hands, as if he needed anything, because he himself gives all men life and breath and everything else.

ACTS 17:24-25 NIV

April 5

$\mathcal{M}$y friends have made the story
of my life. In a thousand ways they
have turned my limitations into beautiful
privileges, and enabled me to walk
serene and happy in the shadow
cast by my deprivation.

HELEN KELLER

April 6

$\mathcal{T}$rue happiness consists not
in the multitude of friends,
but in the worth and choice.

BEN JONSON

When you are young and without success,
you have only a few friends. Then, later on,
when you are rich and famous, you still
have a few...if you are lucky.

PABLO PICASSO

April 7

*A*lways set high value on spontaneous kindness. He whose inclination prompts him to cultivate your friendship of his own accord will love you more than one whom you have been at pains to attach to you.

SAMUEL JOHNSON

April 8

$\mathcal{I}$ have always differentiated between
two types of friends; those who want
proofs of friendship, and those who
do not. One kind loves me for myself,
and the others for themselves.

GERARD DE NERVAL

April 9

I will bless the Lord who guides me;
even at night my heart instructs me.
I know the Lord is always with me.
I will not be shaken, for he is right beside
me. No wonder my heart is filled
with joy, and my mouth shouts his
praises! My body rests in safety.

PSALM 16:7-9 NLT

April 10

The light of God surrounds me,
The love of God enfolds me,
The power of God protects me,
The Presence of God watches over me,
Wherever I am, God is.

April 11

In real friendship the judgment, the
genius, the prudence of each party
becomes the common property of both.

MARIA EDGEWORTH

April 12

Oh, what a cause of thankfulness it is that we have a gracious God to go to on all occasions! Use and enjoy this privilege and you can never be miserable. Oh, what an unspeakable privilege is prayer!

Lady Maxwell

April 13

I know not by what methods rare,
But this I know: God answers prayer.
I know not if the blessing sought
Will come in just the guise I thought.
I leave my prayer to Him alone
Whose will is wiser than my own.

Eliza M. Hickok

April 14

$\mathcal{D}$ear friends, if our hearts do not condemn us, we have confidence before God and receive from him anything we ask, because we obey his commands and do what pleases him. And this is his command: to believe in the name of his Son, Jesus Christ, and to love one another as he commanded us.

1 JOHN 3:21-23

April 15

If one advances confidently in the
direction of his dreams, and endeavors
to live the life which he has imagined,
he will meet with a success
unexpected in common hours.

HENRY DAVID THOREAU

April 16

*I*n comparison with this big world, the human heart is only a small thing. Though the world is so large, it is utterly unable to satisfy this tiny heart. Our ever growing soul and its capacities can be satisfied only in the infinite God. As water is restless until it reaches its level, so the soul has no peace until it rests in God.

SADHU SUNDAR SINGH

April 17

$\mathcal{I}$ am not exactly sure what heaven will be like, but I do know that when we die and it comes time for God to judge us, He will not ask, "How many good things have you done in your life?", rather He will ask, "How much love did you put into what you did?"

MOTHER TERESA

April 18

$\mathcal{I}$f there is light in the soul, there will be beauty in the person. If there is beauty in the person, there will be harmony in the house. If there is harmony in the house, there will be order in the nation. If there is order in the nation, there will be peace in the world.

CHINESE PROVERB

April 19

The Lord is faithful to all his promises and loving toward all he has made.... You open your hand and satisfy the desires of every living thing.

PSALM 145:13-16 NIV

April 20

*H*is thoughts were slow,
His words were few and never
formed to glisten,
But he was a joy to all his friends,
you should have heard him listen!

April 21

$\mathcal{H}$elping others, that's the
main thing. The only way for us
to help ourselves is to help others
and listen to each other's stories.

ELI WIESEL

April 22

Count your blessings, not your troubles. Learn to live one day at a time. Learn to say, "I love you," "thank you," and "I appreciate you." Learn to be a giver and not a getter. Seek the good in everyone and everything. Pray every day.

April 23

$\mathcal{F}$or attractive lips, speak words
of kindness. For beautiful eyes,
seek out the good in other people,
To lose weight, let go of stress and
the need to control others. To improve
your ears, listen to the word of God.
Touch someone with your love.

April 24

Create in me a clean heart, O God.
Renew a right spirit within me.
Do not banish me from your
presence, and don't take your
Holy Spirit from me. Restore to me
again the joy of your salvation,
and make me willing to obey you.

PSALM 51:10-12 NLT

April 25

$\mathcal{H}$ow far you go in life depends
on your being tender with the young,
compassionate with the aged,
sympathetic with the striving,
and tolerant of the weak and strong.
Because someday in your life
you will have been all of these.

GEORGE WASHINGTON CARVER

April 26

$\mathcal{H}$ow many people eat, drink,
and get married; buy, sell, and build;
make contracts and attend to their
fortune, have friends and enemies,
pleasures and pains, are born,
grow up, live and die—but asleep!

JOSEPH JOUBERT

April 27

Live each season as it passes; breathe
the air, drink the drink, taste the fruit, and
resign yourself to the influences of each.

HENRY DAVID THOREAU

April 28

$\mathcal{I}$f I look at myself, I am depressed.
If I look at those around me,
I am often disappointed. If I look
at circumstances, I am discouraged.
But if I look at Jesus, I am constantly,
consistently, and eternally fulfilled!

April 29

The Lord will guide you always;
he will satisfy your needs.... You will
be like a well-watered garden, like
a spring whose waters never fail.

ISAIAH 58:11 NIV

April 30

$\mathcal{A}$ kind heart is a fountain
of gladness, making everything
in its vicinity freshen into smiles.

WASHINGTON IRVING

May 1

$\mathcal{I}$t's funny how a little hug makes
everyone feel good;
In every place and language,
it's always understood.

JILL WOLF

May 2

*L*ove is always open arms. With arms open you allow love to come and go as it will, freely, for it'll do so anyway. If you close your arms about love, you'll find you are left only holding yourself.

May 3

$\mathcal{S}$pread love everywhere you go: First of all in your own house...let no one ever come to you without leaving better and happier. Be the living expression of God's kindness; kindness in your face, kindness in your eyes, kindness in your smile, kindness in your warm greeting.

MOTHER TERESA

May 4

$\mathcal{P}$raise the Lord, all you nations.
Praise him, all you people of the earth.
For he loves us with unfailing love;
the faithfulness of the Lord endures
forever. Praise the Lord!

PSALM 117 NLT

May 5

$\mathcal{H}$ave patience with all things,
but chiefly have patience with yourself.
Do not lose courage in considering
your own imperfections, but instantly
set about remedying them—every day
begin the task anew.

FRANCIS DE SALES

May 6

$\mathcal{U}$nless each day can be looked back upon by an individual as one in which he has had some fun, some joy, some real satisfaction, that day is a loss. Take time to laugh, it is the music of the soul.

May 7

$\mathcal{J}$esus gives us the example
of kindness and gentleness.
He was full of sympathy and affection,
and always loved with mercy.

EMILIE BARNES

May 8

$\mathcal{T}$he good old days were never
that good, believe me. The good new
days are today, and better days are
coming tomorrow. Our greatest
songs are still unsung.

HUBERT H. HUMPHREY

May 9

*L*et him have all your worries
and cares, for he is always thinking
about you and watching
everything that concerns you.

1 PETER 5:7 TLB

May 10

God has given us two hands—one to receive with and the other to give with...We are channels made for giving.

BILLY GRAHAM

May 11

$\mathscr{T}$he sense of wonder at the compassion of God causes one to look at others with the same sense of love and care.

JOHN YATES

May 12

$\mathcal{P}$ride is one of the deadly sins; but it cannot be the pride of a mother in her children, for that is a compound of two cardinal virtues—faith and hope.

CHARLES DICKENS

May 13

Three things grow more precious
with age: old wood to burn, old books
to read, and old friends to enjoy.

May 14

$\mathcal{B}$ut Ruth replied, "Don't urge
me to leave you or to turn back
from you. Where you go I will go, and
where you stay I will stay. Your people
will be my people, and your God my
God.... May the Lord deal with me,
be it ever so severely, if anything
but death separates you and me."

RUTH 1:16-17 NIV

May 15

*M*ay you always find three
welcomes in life, in a garden during
summer, at a fireside during winter,
and whatever the day or season,
in the kind eyes of a friend.

May 16

Though we do not have our Lord with us in bodily presence, we have our neighbor, who, for the ends of love and loving service, is as good as our Lord himself.

TERESA OF AVILA

May 17

There is no principle of the heart
that is more acceptable to God
than a universal, ardent love
for all mankind, which seeks
and prays for their happiness.

WILLIAM LAW

May 18

Joyfulness keeps the heart and face young. A good laugh makes us better friends with ourselves and everybody around us.

ORISON SWETT MARDEN

May 19

Be joyful always; pray continually;
give thanks in all circumstances, for this
is God's will for you in Christ Jesus.
Do not put out the Spirit's fire; do not
treat prophecies with contempt.
Test everything. Hold on to the good.

1 THESSALONIANS 5:16-21 NIV

May 20

*N*ever put off until tomorrow what you can do today, because if you enjoy it today, you can do it again, tomorrow.

You are younger today than you ever will be again. Make use of it for the sake of tomorrow.

May 21

Do you have a place somewhere
to seek the Lord in quiet prayer?
A place for just the Lord and you
to share the way that good friends do?
Lift up your heart and start to pray,
He's always just a prayer away.

May 22

A friendship in which heart speaks
to heart is a gift from God, and
no gift that comes from God
is temporary or occasional.

HENRI J. M. NOUWEN

May 23

The A-Z of Friendship

A friend: Accepts you as you are, Believes in you, Calls you just to say "Hi," Doesn't give up on you, Envisions the whole of you, Forgives your mistakes, Gives unconditionally, Helps you, Invites you over, Just to "be" with you, Keeps you close at heart, Loves you for who you are, Makes a difference in your life, Never judges, Offers support, Picks you up, Quiets your fears, Raises your spirits, Says nice things about you, Tells you the truth when you need to hear it, Understands you, Values you, Walks beside you, eXplains things you don't understand, Yells when you won't listen, and Zaps you back into reality.

May 24

$\mathcal{T}$rue friendship never ought
to conceal what it thinks.

JEROME

Encourage each other to build each other up,
just as you are already doing.

1 THESSALONIANS 5:11 TLB

May 25

Friendship Garden

Plant five rows of "P"eas:
preparedness, promptness,
perseverance, politeness, prayer.
Three rows of squash: Squash gossip,
squash criticism, squash indifference.
Five rows of lettuce: Let us love one
another, Let us be faithful, Let us be loyal,
Let us be unselfish, Let us be truthful.
Three rows of Turnips: Turn up for
church, Turn up with a new idea, Turn up
with the determination to do a better job
tomorrow than you did today.

EUGENIE PRIME

May 26

$\mathcal{D}$o what good you can, and do it solely for God's glory, as free from it yourself as though you did not exist. Ask nothing whatever in return. Done in this way, your works are spiritual and godly.

MEISTER ECKHART

May 27

*L*ive while you live,
the epicure would say,
And seize the pleasures
of the present day;
Live while you live,
the sacred preacher cries,
And give to God each moment as it flies.
Lord, in my views, let both united be:
I live in pleasure when I live to Thee.

DODDERIDGE EPIGRAM

May 28

*O*ne ought, every day at least,
to hear a little song, read a good poem,
see a fine picture and, if possible,
speak a few reasonable words.

GOETHE

May 29

$\mathcal{M}$ary sat at the Lord's feet, listening to what he taught. But Martha was worrying over the big dinner she was preparing. She came to Jesus and said, "Lord, doesn't it seem unfair to you that my sister just sits here while I do all the work? Tell her to come and help me." But the Lord said to her, "My dear Martha, you are so upset over all these details! There is really only one thing worth being concerned about. Mary has discovered it—and I won't take it away from her."

LUKE 10:39-42 NLT

$\mathcal{M}ay$ 30

$\mathcal{L}$ook to this day.... In it lie all the
realities and verities of existence,
the bliss of growth, the splendor of
action, the glory of power. For yesterday
is but a dream and tomorrow is only
a vision. But today, well lived, makes
every yesterday a dream of happiness
and every tomorrow a vision of hope.

SANSKRIT PROVERB

May 31

The most wonderful of all things in life, I believe, is the discovery of another human being with whom one's relationship has a glowing depth, beauty and joy as the years increase. This inner progressiveness of love between two human beings is a most marvelous thing, it cannot be found by looking for it or by passionately wishing for it. It is a sort of Divine accident.

SIR HUGH WALPOLE

June 1

$\mathcal{L}$ord, make me an instrument of thy peace, Where there is hatred, let me sow love; Where there is injury, pardon; Where there is doubt, faith, Where there is despair, hope; Where there is darkness, light; Where there is sadness, joy.

Francis of Assisi

June 2

$\mathcal{A}$ll things are possible to him who believes, yet more to him who hopes, more still to him who loves, and most of all to him who practices and perseveres in these three virtues.

BROTHER LAWRENCE

June 3

The best way to get to know a new friend is to spend time with him, to talk with him. And the best way to get to know God better is to spend time with Him, to talk to Him. That's what prayer is—simply talking to God.

STEPHEN L. SPANOUDIS

June 4

God is love. Whoever lives in love lives in God, and God in him. In this way, love is made complete among us so that we will have confidence on the day of judgment, because in this world we are like him. There is no fear in love.

1 JOHN 4:16-18 NIV

June 5

*W*hen our friends are present we ought to treat them well: and when they are absent, to speak of them well.

EPICTETUS

We must not trust every word of others or feeling within ourselves, but cautiously and patiently try the matter, to see whether it is of God.

THOMAS À KEMPIS

June 6

God puts each fresh morning,
each new chance of life, into our hands
as a gift to see what we will do with it.

June 7

God moves in a mysterious way
His wonders to perform;
He plants His footsteps on the sea,
And rides upon the storm.
Deep in unfathomable mines
Of never-failing skill,
He treasures up His bright designs
And works His sovereign will.
Blind unbelief is sure to err and scan
His work in vain;
God is His own interpreter, and He
will make it plain.

WILLIAM COWPER

June 8

A good friend will sharpen your character, draw your soul into the light, and challenge your heart to love in a greater way.

June 9

*A*im at heaven and you get
earth thrown in; aim at earth
and you get neither.

C.S. LEWIS

Whatever you do, do it with kindness and love.

1 CORINTHIANS 16:14 TLB

June 10

$\mathscr{H}$appiness is found along the way,
not at the end of the road.

Far away in the sunshine are my highest
inspirations. I may not reach them, but
can look up and see the beauty, believe in
them and try to follow where they lead.

LOUISA MAY ALCOTT

June 11

A joyful heart is like the sunshine of
God's love, the hope of eternal happiness.

MOTHER TERESA

*You talk about your pleasures
to your acquaintances; you talk
about your troubles to your friends.*

BROTHER ANDREW

June 12

$\mathcal{I}$ think the purpose of life
is to be useful, to be responsible,
to be honorable, to be compassionate.
It is, after all, to matter: to count,
to stand for something, to have made
some difference that you lived at all.

LEO C. ROSTEN

June 13

*L*ove is something like the clouds that were in the sky before the sun came out. You cannot touch the clouds, you know; but you feel the rain and know how glad the flowers and the thirsty earth are to have it after a hot day. You cannot touch love either; but you feel the sweetness that it pours into everything.

ANNIE SULLIVAN

June 14

*C*hristianity has taught us to care.
Caring is the greatest thing,
caring matters most.

FRIEDRICH VON HUGEL

*Greater love has no one than this,
than to lay down one's life for his friends.*

JOHN 15:13 NKJV

June 15

$\mathcal{T}$he friendship that can cease
has never been real.

JEROME

Every act of kindness and compassion done
by any man for his fellow Christian
is done by Christ working within him.

JULIAN OF NORWICH

June 16

Through thick and thin, what's out, what's in, Through ups and downs and joys and frowns, Friendship is life's giving part; it lives and breathes heart-to-heart.

June 17

*W*henever friendship comes to pass,
it never goes away, For it is born to love
and give, and set two hearts at play.

June 18

*W*orry never climbed a hill, worry never paid a bill, Worry never dried a tear, worry never calmed a fear, Worry never darned a heel, worry never cooked a meal, It never led a horse to water, nor ever did a thing it "oughter."

June 19

$\mathcal{T}$here's no such thing as
a person alone. There are only
people bound to each other
to the limits of humanity and time.

MICHEL QUOIST

He who refreshes others will himself be refreshed.

PROVERBS 11:25 NIV

June 20

*J*oys and sorrows ever blend,
in moments shared with a friend.
Grace and happiness abound
where loving friendship can be found.

June 21

When I was young I was sure of everything; in a few years, having been mistaken a thousand times, I was not half so sure of most things as I was before; at present, I am hardly sure of anything but what God has revealed.

JOHN WESLEY

June 22

Be strong! We are not here to play,
to dream, to drift;
We have hard work to do
and loads to lift;
Shun not the struggle—
face it; 'its God's gift.

MALTBIE D. BABCOCK

June 23

$\mathcal{F}$rom quiet homes and first beginning,
Out to undiscovered ends,
There's nothing worth
the wear of winning,
But laughter
and the love of friends.

HILAIRE BELLOC

$\mathcal{J}$une 24

You are the light of the world. A city on a hill cannot be hidden. Neither do people light a lamp and put it under a bowl. Instead they put it on a stand, and it gives light to everyone in the house. In the same way, let your light shine before men, that they may see your good deeds and praise your Father in heaven.

MATTHEW 5:14-16 NIV

June 25

$\mathcal{N}$ot by chance or circumstance,
do friends meet on the way,
But by Grace, they reach the place
to laugh and share and pray.

*A good friend kindly reminds us
who we are meant to be.*

June 26

$\mathcal{F}$riendship comes when we embrace,
God's gifts of tenderness and Grace,
and when we learn to see each other,
as God's own, His sister and brother.

June 27

*W*hat joy when friends hike
side by side on a summer's day,
And greater still, to top the hill
and settle down to pray.

June 28

A true friend inspires you to believe the best in yourself, to keep pursuing your deepest dreams—most wonderful of all, she celebrates all your successes as if they were her own!

June 29

$\mathcal{F}$riends may not always have the answers, but they're always willing to consider the questions.

Kind words are like honey…enjoyable and healthful.

PROVERBS 16:24 TLB

June 30

$\mathcal{F}$riends always hold
each other in prayer.

If we would build on a sure foundation
in friendship, we must love our friends
for their sakes rather than our own.

CHARLOTTE BRONTË

$\mathcal{J}uly$ 1

Good friends love us when
we're strong,
Great friends love us when we're wrong,
True friends guide us back to right,
Real friends hold us in God's Light.

July 2

*W*hat a friend we have in Jesus,
all our sins and griefs to bear,
What a privilege to carry
everything to God in prayer.

H Y M N

July 3

$\mathcal{B}$uds of friendship open wide,
revealing beauty deep inside.

If I had a single flower for every time I think
of you, I could walk forever in my garden.

CLAUDIA A. GRAND

July 4

There is blessing in the sunshine,
blessing in the rain, blessing
in the lessons
that sometimes bring us pain,
There is blessing in the giving
and in the things we lend,
But perhaps the dearest blessing
is in discovering a friend.

From the fullness of his grace we have
all received one blessing after another.

John 1:16 niv

July 5

Of all the things that two friends do,
to create a bond that's warm and true,
The greatest comes as they are living,
learning, growing and forgiving.

July 6

Budding friends, like flowers bloom,
When they're given growing room.
Lasting friends, in joy remain,
By deeds they plant in sun and rain.

July 7

$\mathcal{W}$ays to be good to yourself:
Be yourself—truthfully,
accept yourself—gracefully,
value yourself—joyfully,
forgive yourself—completely,
treat yourself—generously,
balance yourself—harmoniously,
bless yourself—abundantly,
trust yourself—confidently,
love yourself—wholeheartedly.

July 8

*W*e are all weak, finite, simple human beings, standing in the need of prayer. None need it so much as those who think they are strong, those who know it not, but are deluded by self-sufficiency.

HAROLD C. PHILLIPS

July 9

*O*nly love can be divided endlessly
and still not diminish.

ANNE MORROW LINDBERGH

*See to it that you really do love each
other warmly, with all your hearts.*

1 PETER 1:22 TLB

July 10

*O*ne friend in a lifetime is much;
two are many; three are hardly possible.

HENRY ADAMS

To find a friend one must close one eye.
To keep him—two.

NORMAN DOUGLAS

July 11

$\mathcal{T}$he Serenity Prayer: God grant me the serenity to accept things I cannot change; the courage to change things I can and wisdom to know the difference.

REINHOLD NIEBUHR

July 12

I sought my soul,
But my soul I could not see.
I sought my God, But my God eluded me.
I sought my brother,
And I found all three.

July 13

Say well is good, but do well is better;
Do well seems the spirit,
say well the letter;
Say well is godly
and helps to please,
But do well is godly
and gives the world ease.

July 14

In thought, faith; In word, wisdom;
In deed, courage; In life, service.

*If anyone serves, he should do it with the strength
God provides, so that in all things God may
be praised through Jesus Christ. To him be the
glory and the power for ever and ever. Amen.*

1 PETER 4:11 NIV

July 15

*H*appiness…consists in giving,
and in serving others.

HENRY DRUMMOND

*Every charitable act is a stepping
stone toward heaven.*

HENRY WARD BEECHER

July 16

A good friend is better
than silver and gold.

DUTCH PROVERB

Goodness is the only investment that never fails.

HENRY DAVID THOREAU

July 17

The most eloquent prayer is the prayer through hands that heal and bless. The highest form of worship is the worship of unselfish Christian service. The greatest form of praise is the sound of the consecrated feet seeking out the lost and helpless.

BILLY GRAHAM

July 18

If I can stop one heart from breaking,
I shall not live in vain;
If I can ease one life the aching,
Or cool one pain,
Or help one fainting robin unto his
nest again,
I shall not live in vain.

EMILY DICKINSON

July 19

$\mathcal{B}$e devoted to one another in brotherly love. Honor one another above yourselves. Never be lacking in zeal, but keep your spiritual fervor, serving the Lord. Be joyful in hope, patient in affliction, faithful in prayer. Share with God's people who are in need. Practice hospitality.

ROMANS 12:10-13 NIV

July 20

$\mathcal{P}$urity of heart and simplicity
are of great force with almighty God,
who is in purity most singular,
and of nature most simple.

GREGORY THE GREAT

July 21

$\mathcal{W}$e must not hope to be mowers,
And to gather the ripe old ears,
Unless we have first been sowers
And watered the furrows with tears.
It is not just as we take it,
This mystical world of ours,
Life's field will yield as we make it
A harvest of thorns or of flowers.

GOETHE

July 22

$\mathcal{A}$ visitor saw a nurse attending the sores of a leprosy patient. "I would not do that for a million dollars," she said. The nurse answered, "Neither would I, but I do it for Jesus for nothing."

CORRIE TEN BOOM

July 23

*T*here is nothing on this earth more
to be prized than true friendship.

THOMAS AQUINAS

July 24

Trust in the Lord with all your heart
and lean not on your own understanding;
in all your ways acknowledge him,
and he will make your paths straight.

PROVERBS 3:5-6 NIV

July 25

Remember that there must be
someone to cook the meals,
and count yourselves happy in being
able to serve like Martha.

TERESA OF AVILA

*I know what things are good: friendship
and work and conversation.*

RUPERT BROOKE

July 26

For there is no friend like a sister
in calm and stormy weather;
To cheer one on the tedious way,
To fetch one if one goes astray,
To lift one if one totters down,
To strengthen whilst one stands.

CHRISTINA ROSSETTI

July 27

*L*et us make one point…that we
meet each other with a smile, when it is
difficult to smile…. Smile at each other,
make time for each other in your family.

MOTHER TERESA

July 28

$\mathcal{T}$rue happiness…arises, in the first place, from the enjoyment of one's self, and in the next from the friendship and conversation of a few select companions.

JOSEPH ADDISON

July 29

*W*ithout friends, no one would choose
to live, though he had all other goods.

ARISTOTLE

*Love knows no limit to its endurance,
no end to its trust, no fading of its hope;
it can outlast anything.*

1 CORINTHIANS 13:8 PHILIPS

July 30

$\mathcal{F}$riendship is an art,
and very few persons are
born with a natural gift for it.

KATHLEEN NORRIS

*Friendship is the only cement that
will ever hold the world together.*

WOODROW WILSON

July 31

*G*od is able to make a way out
of no way and transform dark
yesterdays into bright tomorrows.
This is our hope for becoming better
men and women. This is our mandate
for seeking to make a better world.

MARTIN LUTHER KING JR

August 1

$\mathcal{W}$hat you can do, or dream you can,
begin it. Boldness has genius,
power and magic in it. Only engage,
and then the mind grows heated;
Begin it and the task will be completed.

GOETHE

August 2

$\mathcal{W}$atch your thoughts;
they become words. Watch your words;
they become actions. Watch your actions;
they become habits. Watch your habits;
they become character. Watch your
character; for it becomes your destiny!

August 3

$\mathcal{T}$each me to find another's woe,
  To hide the fault I see;
That mercy I to others show,
  That mercy show to me.

ALEXANDER POPE

August 4

God is our Light and our Protector.
He gives us grace and glory.
No good thing will he withhold from
those who walk along his paths.

PSALM 84:11 TLB

August 5

The life of the spirit is centrally and essentially a life of action. Spirituality is something done, not merely believed, or known or experienced.

MARY McDERMOTT SHIDELER

August 6

On God for all events depend;
You cannot want when God's your friend.
Weigh well your part and do your best;
Leave to your Maker all the rest.

NATHANIEL COTTON

August 7

Be not dismayed at the troubles of the earth. Tremble not at the convulsions of empires. Only, fear God; only believe in his promises; only love and serve him; and all things shall work together for thy good, as they assuredly will for his glory.

<small>SPIRITUAL EXERCISES OF THE HEART</small>

August 8

When I don't know why,
I simply must,
Go to God in childlike trust,
When I don't know what
to think or say,
I simply go to Him and pray.

August 9

$\mathcal{L}$ove has its source in God, for love
is the very essence of His being.

KAY ARTHUR

You have welcomed me as your guest;
blessings overflow! Your goodness and unfailing
kindness shall be with me all of my life.

PSALM 23:5-6 TLB

August 10

$\mathcal{A}$n act of love that fails is just as much a part of the divine life as an act of love that succeeds, for love is measured by its own fullness, not by its reception.

HAROLD LOUKES

Actions, not words, are the true criterion of the attachment of friends.

GEORGE WASHINGTON

August 11

They might not need me; but they might. I'll let my head be just in sight; A smile as small as mine might be Precisely their necessity.

EMILY DICKINSON

August 12

The young people of today think of nothing but themselves. They have not reverence for parents or old age. They are impatient of all restraint. They talk as if they know everything, and what passes for wisdom with us is foolishness to them.

PETER THE MONK, 1274

August 13

There can be no friendship when there is no freedom. Friendship loves the free air, and will not be fenced up in straight and narrow enclosures.

WILLIAM PENN

August 14

$\mathcal{F}$orgive, and you will be forgiven.
Give, and it will be given to you.
A good measure, pressed down, shaken
together and running over, will be poured
into your lap. For with the measure you
use, it will be measured to you.

LUKE 6:37-38 NIV

August 15

$\mathcal{J}$oys come from simple and natural things: mists over meadows, sunlight on leaves, the path of the moon over water.

SIGURD F. OLSON

August 16

Givers can be divided into three types:
the flint, the sponge and the honeycomb.
Some givers are like a piece of flint—to
get anything out of it you must hammer
it, and even then you only get chips and
sparks. Others are like a sponge—to get
anything out of the sponge you must
squeeze it and squeeze it hard,
because the more you squeeze
a sponge, the more you get. But others
are like a honeycomb—which just
overflows with its own sweetness.
That is how God gives to us,
and it is how we should give in turn.

August 17

*H*e who is gentle remembers
good rather than evil, the good
one has received rather than
the good one has done.

ARISTOTLE

*The best rule of friendship is to keep
your heart a little softer than your head.*

August 18

A Christian should always remember that the value of his good works is not based on their numbers and excellence, but on the love of God which prompts him to do these things.

JOHN OF THE CROSS

August 19

$\mathcal{T}$hey are rich who have true friends.

THOMAS FULLER

The Lord's blessing is our greatest wealth.

PROVERBS 10:22 TLB

August 20

I wish you love, and strength,
and faith, and wisdom,
Goods, gold enough to help
some needy one.
I wish you songs, but also blessed
silence,
And God's sweet peace
when every day is done.

Dorothy Nell McDonald

August 21

$\mathcal{F}$riendship, of itself a holy tie,
is made more sacred by adversity.

JOHN DRYDEN

August 22

*A*ll that is good, all that is true,
all that is beautiful, all that is beneficent,
be it great or small, be it perfect
or fragmentary, natural as well
as supernatural, moral as well
as material, comes from God.

JOHN HENRY NEWMAN

August 23

*L*ittle drops of water,
little grains of sand,
Make the mighty ocean,
and the pleasant land:
So the little minutes,
humble though they be,
Make the mighty ages of eternity.
Little deeds of kindness,
little words of love,
Help to make earth happy,
like Heaven up above.

JULIA CARNEY

August 24

*I*f you love someone you will
be loyal to him no matter what the cost.
You will always believe in him, always
expect the best of him, and always
stand your ground in defending him.

1 CORINTHIANS 13:7 TLB

August 25

The smallest effort is not lost,
Each wavelet on the ocean tossed
Aids in the ebb-tied or the flow,
Each raindrop makes some floweret
blow; Each struggle lessens human woe.

CHARLES MACKAY

August 26

$\mathcal{B}$e of good cheer. Do not think
of today's failures, but of the success
that may come tomorrow. You have set
yourselves a difficult task, but you will
succeed if you persevere; and you will
find a joy in overcoming obstacles.
Remember, no effort that we make to
attain something beautiful is ever lost.

HELEN KELLER

August 27

$\mathcal{I}$n your journeys to and fro
God direct you;
In your happiness and pleasure,
God bless you;
In care, anxiety or trouble,
God sustain you;
In peril and danger, God protect you.

TIMOTHY OLUFOSOYE

August 28

To be capable of steady friendship
or lasting love are the two greatest
proofs, not only of goodness of heart,
but of strength of mind.

WILLIAM HAZLITT

August 29

How I thank God through Jesus Christ for each one of you. God knows how often I pray for you. Day and night I bring you and your needs in prayer to God, whom I serve with all my heart by telling others the Good News about his Son.

ROMANS 1:8-9 NLT

August 30

$\mathcal{W}$atch, dear Lord, with those who wake, or watch, or weep tonight, and give your angels charge over those who sleep. Tend your sick ones, O Lord Christ, rest your weary ones. Bless your dying ones. Soothe your suffering ones. Pity your afflicted ones. Shield your joyous ones. And all for your love's sake. Amen.

AUGUSTINE

August 31

*L*ord, today you have made
us known to friends we did not know,
and you have given us seats in homes
which are not our own. You have
brought the distant near, and made
a brother of a stranger. Forgive us
Lord…we did not introduce you.

POLYNESIAN PRAYER

September 1

Charity is, indeed, a great thing, and a gift of God, and when it is rightly ordered likens us unto God Himself, as far as that is possible; for it is charity which makes the person.

JOHN CHRYSOSTOM

September 2

$\mathcal{C}$hrist cannot live His life today in this
world without our mouth, without our
eyes, without our going and coming,
without our heart. When we love,
it is Christ loving through us.

CARDINAL SUENENS

September 3

*M*ay you have warm words
on a cold evening, a full moon
on a dark night, and the road downhill
all the way to your door.

September 4

*A*biding love surrounds those who
trust in the Lord. So rejoice in him,
all those who are his, and shout for joy,
all those who try to obey him.

PSALM 32:10-11 TLB

September 5

It's the little things we do and say
that mean so much as we go our way.
A kindly deed can lift a load
from weary shoulders on the road.

WILLA HOEY

September 6

God writes the gospel not
in the Bible alone, but on trees
and flowers and clouds and stars.

MARTIN LUTHER

September 7

$\mathcal{F}$or memory has painted this
perfect day with colors that never fade.
And we find at the end of the day,
the soul of a friend we've made.

CARRIE JACOBS BOND

September 8

$\mathcal{T}$here is a grace of kind listening,
as well as a grace of kind speaking.

FREDERICK W. FABER

*Fix your thoughts on what is true and good and
right. Think about things that are pure and lovely,
and dwell on the fine, good things in others.*

PHILIPPIANS 4:8 TLB

September 9

*N*ever ending, still beginning,
Fighting still, and still destroying,
If all the world be worth the winning,
Think, oh think, it worth enjoying.

JOHN DRYDEN

September 10

$\mathcal{F}$riendships begun in this world can be taken up again in heaven, never to be broken off.

FRANCIS DE SALES

Sweet is the memory of distant friends!

WASHINGTON IRVING

September 11

Try as hard as you like, but in the end only the language of the heart can ever reach another's heart while mere words, as they slip from your tongue, don't get past your listener's ear.

FRANCIS DE SALES

September 12

A cheerful giver does not count the cost of what he gives. His heart is set on pleasing and cheering him to whom the gift is given.

JULIAN OF NORWICH

September 13

*C*hristians are the only people
in the world who have anything
to be happy about.

BILLY GRAHAM

September 14

A good deed is never lost;
he who sows courtesy reaps friendship,
and he who plants kindness gathers love.

Basil

*A friend is always loyal, and a brother
is born to help in time of need.*

Proverbs 17:17 NLT

September 15

*M*other to six year old: "Jane, what are you doing?"
"I'm drawing God."
"But darling, nobody knows what God looks like."
"No, mummy, they don't YET, but they will when they've seen my drawing."

ROBERT LLEWELYN

September 16

*O*h! Be thou blest with what heaven can send,
Long health, long youth, long pleasure, and a friend!

ALEXANDER POPE

September 17

$\mathcal{T}$rue joy is the earnest wish we have of heaven, it is a treasure of the soul, and therefore should be laid in a safe place, and nothing in this world is safe to place it in.

JOHN DONNE

September 18

$\mathcal{T}$he best portion of a good person's life, the little nameless, unremembered acts of kindness and of love.

WILLIAM WORDSWORTH

September 19

$\mathcal{T}$he hands of a friend are gentle,
and the heart is always open.

*The Lord your God. will take great delight
in you, he will quiet you with his love,
he will rejoice over you with singing.*

ZEPHANIAH 3:17 NIV

September 20

*H*ope is not a granted wish
or a favor performed; no, it is far greater
than that. It is a zany, unpredictable
dependence on a God who loves
to surprise us out of our socks.

MAX LUCADO

September 21

$\mathcal{T}$he good for which we are born into
this world is that we may learn to love.

GEORGE MacDONALD

True happiness consists not in the multitude
of friends, but in the worth and choice.

BEN JONSON

September 22

*Y*our life unfolds in a continuous succession of experience and expectations…Every day has enough trouble of its own. When you go to sleep, bury all that has happened in the mercy of God. It will be safe there. Stand back from what has happened and be grateful for it all.

September 23

Our life is love, and peace,
and tenderness; and bearing
one with another, and forgiving
one another, and not laying
accusations one against another.

Isaac Penington

September 24

$\mathcal{F}$riendships last when
they are put first.

Dear friends, since God so loved us,
we also ought to love one another.

1 JOHN 4:11 NIV

September 25

$\mathcal{F}$riends always listen from the heart.

*Half an hour's listening is essential
except when you are very busy.
Then a full hour is needed.*

FRANCIS DE SALES

September 26

$\mathcal{W}$e can make up our minds whether our lives in this world shall wound like thorns and nettles, or be beautiful and fragrant like the lilies of the field.

BROTHER ANDREW

September 27

$\mathcal{L}$ove is the most durable power in the world. This creative force, so beautifully exemplified in the life of our Christ, is the most potent instrument available in mankind's quest for peace and security.

September 28

$\mathcal{I}$ always prefer to believe
the best of everybody.

RUDYARD KIPLING

*The highest love of all finds its fulfillment
not in what it keeps, but in what it gives.*

BROTHER ANDREW

September 29

$\mathcal{N}$o life is so strong or complete,
But it yearns for the smile of a friend.

WALLACE BRUCE

*I have called you friends, for everything
that I learned from my Father
I have made known to you.*

JOHN 15:15 NIV

September 30

$\mathcal{F}$riends come in,
when all others leave.

*Friendship is a union of spirits, a marriage of
hearts, and the bond there of virtue.*

October 1

$\mathcal{I}$t is His long-term policy, I fear, to restore to them a new kind of self-love—a charity and gratitude for all selves including their own; when they have really learned to love their neighbours as themselves, they will be allowed to love themselves as their neighbours.

C. S. LEWIS

October 2

*W*ere the whole realm of nature mine,
That were an offering far too small;
Love so amazing, so Divine,
Demands my soul, my life, my all.

ISAAC WATTS

October 3

The corn that makes the holy bread
By which the soul of man is fed,
The holy bread, the food unpriced,
Thy everlasting mercy, Christ.

JOHN MASEFIELD

October 4

*W*hen we love each other
God lives in us, and his love
within us grows ever stronger.

1 JOHN 4:12 TLB

October 5

$\mathcal{I}$ have friends in overalls whose
friendship I would not swap for
the favor of the kings of the world.

THOMAS A. EDISON

October 6

$\mathcal{F}$riendship with oneself is all
important, because without it one
cannot be friends with anyone else.

ELEANOR ROOSEVELT

October 7

$\mathcal{I}$ desire so to conduct the affairs of this administration that if at the end...I have lost every other friend on earth, I shall at least have one friend left, and that friend shall be down inside of me.

ABRAHAM LINCOLN

October 8

*H*e prayeth well, who loveth well
Both man and bird and beast.
He prayeth best, who loveth best
All things both great and small;
For the dear God who loveth us,
He made and loveth all.

SAMUEL TAYLOR COLERIDGE

October 9

*G*od is more anxious to bestow
his blessings on us than we
are to receive them.

AUGUSTINE

*Many blessings are given
to those who trust the Lord.*

PSALM 40:4 TLB

October 10

A good friend puts up with
your worst moods, goes along
with your worst ideas,
and always sees the best in you.

Barbara Johnson

October 11

$\mathcal{A}$ friend is a present you give yourself.

ROBERT LOUIS STEVENSON

A friend is someone you can
do nothing with, and enjoy it.

October 12

That perfect devoting ourselves to God, from which devotion has its name, requires that we should not only do the will of God, but also that we should do it with love. "He loveth a cheerful giver," and without the heart no obedience is acceptable to Him.

FRANCOIS FÉNELON

October 13

Two friends—two bodies
with one soul inspired.

HOMER

The soul is in itself a most lovely and perfect
image of God.

JOHN OF THE CROSS

October 14

*I*n poverty and other misfortunes of life, true friends are a sure refuge.

ARISTOTLE

My God will meet all your needs according to his glorious riches.

PHILIPPIANS 4:19 NIV

October 15

$\mathcal{T}$he fruit of silence is prayer.
The fruit of prayer is faith. The fruit of
faith is love. The fruit of love is service.
The fruit of service is peace.

MOTHER TERESA

October 16

Self-discipline never means giving up everything, for giving up is a loss. Our Lord did not ask us to give up the things of earth, but to exchange them for better things.

FULTON J. SHEEN

October 17

*G*reat works do not always
lie in our way, but every
moment we may do little ones
excellently, that is, with great love.

FRANCIS DE SALES

October 18

$\mathcal{A}$ real friend helps us think
our best thoughts, do our noblest
deeds, be our finest selves.
The real friend is he or she who can
share all our sorrow and double our joys.

B.C. FORBES

October 19

$\mathcal{A}$ pleasant companion reduces
the length of a journey.

SYRUS

Be truly glad! There is wonderful joy ahead.

1 PETER 1:6 TLB

October 20

O most merciful Redeemer,
Friend and Brother,
May we know Thee more clearly,
Love Thee more dearly,
Follow Thee more nearly:
For ever and ever.

RICHARD OF CHICHESTER

October 21

$\mathcal{I}$f you laugh a lot, when
you get older your wrinkles
will be in the right places.

A N D R E W M A S O N

October 22

$\mathcal{D}$o not protect yourself by a fence,
but rather by your friends.

CZECH PROVERB

In reality, we are all still children. We want
to find a playmate for our thoughts and feelings.

WILHELM STEKHEL

October 23

$\mathcal{G}$od is the friend of silence.
Trees, flowers, grass grow in silence.
See the stars, moon and sun
how they move in silence.

MOTHER TERESA

October 24

$\mathcal{P}$erfume and incense bring
joy to the heart, and the
pleasantness of one's friend
springs from his earnest counsel.

Proverbs 27:9 niv

October 25

The kindling power of our words
must not come from outward show
but from within, not from oratory
but straight from the heart.

FRANCIS DE SALES

October 26

*W*ho is the third who walks
always beside you?
When I count,
there are only you and I together.
But when I look ahead up the
white road
There is always another
one walking beside you.

T. S. ELIOT

October 27

$\mathcal{I}$ believe sympathy is one
of the most helpful helps one can
bestow upon one's fellow creatures;
and it seems a great pity that so
many people feel it is their duty to
criticize rather than sympathize.

Hannah Whithall Smith

October 28

$\mathcal{K}$nowing what to say is not always necessary; just the presence of a caring friend can make a world of difference.

SHERI CURRY

October 29

The test of enjoyment is the remembrance which it leaves behind.

LOGAN PEARSALL SMITH

Greater love hath no man than this,
that a man lay down his life for his friends.

I JOHN 15:13 KJV

October 30

$\mathcal{L}$ord, grant that I may seek
to comfort rather than be comforted;
to love rather than to be loved.

Mother Teresa

October 31

$\mathcal{T}$he world is so full of a number
of things, I'm sure we should
all be as happy as kings.

ROBERT LOUIS STEVENSON

November 1

*L*ord, Your name is Love. In Your love there is sweetness beyond words. Grant that I may always be faithful to my friends here on earth, that I may be worthy of Your faithful love for me.

JOHN SERGIEFF

November 2

$\mathcal{F}$our be the things I am wiser
to know: Idleness, sorrow,
a friend, and a foe.

*The grand essentials to happiness
in this life are something to do, something
to love and something to hope for.*

JOSEPH ADDISON

November 3

$\mathcal{R}$eflect on God's gifts:
My list includes good health,
harmonious family, sufficient food,
clothing, shelter. Friends. Great job.
In light of God's magnificent grace,
a cheerful heart and openhanded
generosity seem the most
natural responses.

CHARLES SWINDOLL

$\mathcal{N}$ovember 4

*A*sk, and you will be given what
you ask for. Seek, and you will find.
Knock, and the door will be opened.
For everyone who asks, receives.
Anyone who seeks, finds. If only
you will knock, the door will open.

MATTHEW 7:7-8 TLB

November 5

God gives us joy that we may give;
He gives us joy that we may share;
Sometimes He gives us loads to lift
That we may learn to bear.
For life is gladder when we give,
And love is sweeter when we share,
And heavy loads rest lightly too
When we have learned to bear.

November 6

$\mathcal{L}$ife is made up, not of great sacrifices
or duties, but of little things, in which
smiles, and kindnesses, and small
obligations, given habitually,
are what win and preserve
the heart and secure comfort.

November 7

One of the secrets of a good friendship
is the ability to accept the storms.

ALAN LOY McGINNIS

November 8

$\mathcal{L}$ook around you, first in your own
family, then among your friends
and neighbors, and see whether
there be not someone whose little
burden you can lighten, whose little
cares you may lessen, whose little
pleasures you can promote, whose
little wants and wishes you can gratify.

LITTLE THINGS, 1852

November 9

I have loved you with
an everlasting love; I have drawn
you with loving-kindness.

JEREMIAH 31:3 NIV

November 10

$\mathcal{F}$rom the simple seeds of understanding, we reap the lovely harvest of true friendship. The best fruits are plucked for each by some hand that is not her own.

C. S. Lewis

November 11

*G*oodness is love in action,
love with its hand on the plow,
love with the burden on its back,
love following His footsteps who
went about continually doing good.

JAMES HAMILTON

November 12

The blessing of a loving friend can't
be over-rated,
The ways a friend can strengthen life
cannot be fully stated.
And so it is with awe and grace
we form an attitude,
Of thankfulness for friendship's
gifts with loving gratitude.

November 13

Faith, hope, and charity—if we had more of the first two, we'd need less of the last.

Let us then be up and doing,
With a heart for any fate,
Still achieving, still pursuing,
Learn to labor and to wait.

HENRY WADSWORTH LONGFELLOW.

November 14

$\mathcal{G}$ive thanks to the Lord,
for he is good; His love and
his kindness go on forever.

1 CHRONICLES 16:34 TLB

November 15

$\mathcal{T}$he miles pass more swiftly,
Taken in a joyous stride,
And all the world seems brighter,
When friends walk by our side.

November 16

*E*ven Jesus didn't try to walk
the earth alone,
He gathered friends about Him
that He could call His own,
And as we walk the earth today,
we're thankful for the part,
That friendship plays in special ways
of sharing heart-to-heart.

November 17

$\mathcal{F}$riendship is something that raises us almost above humanity.... It is the sort of love one can imagine between angels.

C. S. LEWIS

November 18

$\mathcal{I}$t is always possible to be thankful for what is given rather than to complain about what is not given. One or the other becomes a habit of life.

ELISABETH ELLIOT

November 19

The steadfast love of the Lord never ceases, his mercies never come to an end; they are new every morning; great is your faithfulness.

LAMENTATIONS 3:22-23 NRSV

November 20

It was only a sunny smile,
And little it cost in the giving,
But like morning light,
   it scattered the night,
And made the day worth living.

November 21

Gratitude...can turn a meal into a feast, a house into a home, a stranger into a friend. It turns problems into gifts, failures into successes, the unexpected into perfect timing, and mistakes into important events.

MELODY BEATTIE

November 22

There's a miracle called friendship
That dwells within the heart,
And you don't know how it happens
Or where it got its start.
But the happiness it brings you
Always gives a special lift,
And you realize that friendship
Is life's most precious gift.

November 23

$\mathcal{I}$t is not how much you do but how much love you put into the doing and sharing with others that is important. Try not to judge people. If you judge others then you are not giving love. Instead, try to help them by seeing their needs and acting to meet them.

MOTHER TERESA

November 24

$\mathcal{B}$e beautiful inside, in your hearts,
with the lasting charm of a gentle and
quiet spirit which is precious to God.

1 Peter 3:4 tlb

November 25

$\mathcal{Y}$our greatest pleasure is that
which rebounds from hearts
that you have made glad.

Henry Ward Beecher

November 26

$\mathcal{T}$o be grateful is to recognize
the love of God in everything
He has given us and He has
given us everything. Every breath
we draw is a gift of His love.

THOMAS MERTON

November 27

A friend is one who joyfully
sings with you when you are
on the mountain top, and silently
walks beside you through the valley.

WILLIAM A. WARD

November 28

There is nourishment from being encouraged and held up by others when we are weak. We are nourished by feedback from friends whom we trust and who will be honest with us.

RICHARD G. BUHLER

November 29

$\mathcal{A}$ friend is one who believes in you
before you believe in yourself.

Let love be your greatest aim.

1 CORINTHIANS 14:1 TLB

November 30

*Indeed, we do not really live unless we
have friends surrounding us like a firm
wall against the winds of the world.*

CHARLES HANSON TOWNE

December 1

$\mathcal{S}$o long as we love, we serve;
so long as we are loved by others,
I should say that we are almost
indispensable; and no man
is useless while he has a friend.

ROBERT LOUIS STEVENSON

December 2

$\mathcal{G}$ood humor is a tonic for mind and body. It is the best antidote for anxiety and depression. It is a business asset. It attracts and keeps friends. It lightens human burdens It is the direct route to serenity and contentment.

GRENVILLE KLEISER

December 3

$\mathcal{W}$hat shall I bestow upon a friend?
Fleeting moments of silent blessings;
trust in tomorrow, which is life's
hardest task; faith that each new
dawn brings daylight's golden
pathway to the ever-open door;
and a belief that God will be with
them though all others go their way.

LEA PALMER

December 4

*E*very good and perfect gift is from above, coming down from the Father of the heavenly lights, who does not change like shifting shadows.

JAMES 1:17 NIV

December 5

$\mathcal{T}$here is joy in heaven when
a tear of sorrow is shed
in the presence of a truly
understanding heart.
And heaven will
never forget that joy.

CHARLES MALIK

December 6

$\mathcal{N}$o love, no friendship can
cross the path of our destiny without
leaving some mark on it forever.

FRANÇOIS MAURIAC

$\mathcal{D}$ecember 7

$\mathcal{F}$riends are an indispensable part of a meaningful life. They are the ones who share our burdens and multiply our blessings. A true friend sticks by us in our joys and sorrows. In good times and bad, we need friends who will pray for us, listen to us, and lend a comforting hand.

BEVERLY LAHAYE

December 8

Oh, the comfort, the inexpressible comfort of feeling safe with a person: having neither to weigh thoughts nor measure words, but to pour them out.

DINAH MARIA MULOCK CRAIK

December 9

$\mathcal{I}$n God's wisdom, He frequently
chooses to meet our needs
by showing His love toward us through
the hands and hearts of others.

JACK HAYFORD

His joy is in those who reverence him,
those who expect him to be loving and kind.

PSALM 147:11 TLB

December 10

$\mathcal{T}$he unthankful heart...discovers no
mercies; but the thankful heart...will find,
in every hour, some heavenly blessings

HENRY WARD BEECHER

December 11

$\mathcal{T}$he world is a great mirror.
It reflects back to you what you are.
If you are loving, if you are friendly,
if you are helpful, the world will prove
loving and friendly and helpful to you.

THOMAS DREIER

December 12

$\mathcal{I}$f you can help anybody even a little,
be glad; up the steps of usefulness
and kindness, God will lead you
on to happiness and friendship.

Maltbie D. Babcock

December 13

Don't ever let yourself get so busy that you miss those little but important extras in life—the beauty of a day...the smile of a friend...the serenity of a quiet moment alone. For it is often life's smallest pleasures and gentlest joys that make the biggest and most lasting difference.

December 14

*A*re you tired? Worn out? Burned out
on religion? Come to me. Get away with
me and you'll recover your life. I'll show
you how to take a real rest. Walk with
me and work with me—watch how
I do it. Learn the unforced rhythms
of grace.... Keep company with me and
you'll learn to live freely and lightly.

MATTHEW 11: 28-30 THE MESSAGE

December 15

$\mathcal{F}$eeling grateful or appreciative of someone or something in your life actually attracts more of the things that you appreciate and value into your life. And, the more of your life that you like and appreciate, the healthier you'll be.

CHRISTINE NORTHRUP

$\mathcal{D}ecember$ 16

$\mathcal{A}$ friend is someone who understands
your past, believes in your future, and
accepts you today just the way you are.

BEVERLY LaHAYE

December 17

$\mathcal{I}$ still find each day too short
for all the thoughts I want to think,
all the walks I want to take,
all the books I want to read,
and all the friends I want to see.
The longer I live, the more
my mind dwells upon the
beauty and wonder of the world.

JOHN BURROUGHS

December 18

Behind every joyful Christmas
season are busy hands and loving
hands that make the memories
and then pack it all up for the next
year when once again they'll have the
joy of unpacking the memories again.

SANDY LYMAN CLOUGH

December 19

*B*ehold, a virgin shall be with child,
and shall bring forth a son, and they
shall call his name Emmanuel, which
being interpreted is, God with us.

MATTHEW 1:23 KJV

December 20

$\mathcal{M}$ay no gift be too small to give, nor too simple to receive, which is wrapped in thoughtfulness and tied with love.

L. O. BAIRD

$\mathcal{D}ecember$ 21

'*T*is a gift to be simple,
'tis a gift to be free.
'Tis a gift to come round
to where we ought to be.
And when we find a place
that feels just right,
We will be in the valley
of love and delight.

APPALACHIAN FOLK SONG

December 22

*M*any merry Christmases,
many happy New Years.
Unbroken friendships,
great accumulations
of cheerful recollections
and affections on earth,
and heaven for us all.

CHARLES DICKENS

December 23

$\mathcal{F}$or somehow, not only at Christmas,
   but all the long year through,
   the joy that you give to others
   is the joy that comes back to you.

JOHN GREENLEAF WHITTIER

December 24

*F*or to us a child is born, to us a son
is given, and the government will be
on his shoulders. And he will be called
Wonderful Counselor, Mighty God,
Everlasting Father, Prince of Peace.

Isaiah 9:6 niv

December 25

$\mathcal{T}$o be grateful is to recognize the love of God in everything He has given us — and He has given us everything. Every breath we draw is a gift of His love, every moment of existence a gift of grace.

Thomas Merton

December 26

I see friends shaking hands—"How do you do?" They're really saying, "I love you." And I think to myself, "What a wonderful world."

WEISS AND THEILE

December 27

*W*e cannot rebuild the world
by ourselves, but we can have
a small part in it by beginning
where we are. It may only be
taking care of a neighbor's
child or inviting someone
to dinner, but it's all important.

DONNA L. GLAZIER

December 28

$\mathcal{I}$ wish you sunshine on your path
and storms to season your journey.
I wish you peace—in the world
in which you live and in the smallest
corner of the heart where truth
is kept. I wish you faith to help
define your living and your life.
More I cannot wish you—except perhaps
love—to make all the rest worthwhile.

ROBERT A. WARD

December 29

The will of God will not take you
where the grace of God cannot keep you.

Dress in the wardrobe God picked out for you:
compassion, kindness, humility,
quiet strength, discipline.

COLOSSIANS 3:12 THE MESSAGE

December 30